SHITHEAD LAUREATE

HOMELESS

T0163943

CL◀SH

SHITHEAD LAUREATE

Hello.

I am Homeless.

Soon your head will be my home.

No…

Your head is already my home.

My thoughts are inside of you as you read this.

Therefore, I am inside of you now. Living inside you.
Walking around in my boxer briefs. Scratching my balls.
Rearranging the mental furniture inside your head.
Opening the space up in case I feel like entertaining.

I plan on entertaining.

Thank you for letting me live inside your head.

Thank you for giving me a warm place to stay.

At least for now.

I am Homeless.

Hello.

Hello…

The morning sky's
cold, gray coffee breath
ties me down to a park bench
as warped as a melting bathtub
& forces me to watch all of the
21st century bacteria
staring at their phones
in a pathetic, unending search
for fast love
& easy, slut-like validation

& the really fucked up thing
is I used to think it was my fault
I felt so alone all the time.

The change jingled in his cup
like sleigh bells ripped off
Rudolph's shotgunned corpse.
But he was still smiling
at people.

& waving.

He had a shy, grateful
madness in his eyes.

He was the most beautiful creature
I'd ever seen.

Like a housing-impaired,
male version
of Marilyn Monroe.

Eye contact
feels like a bear trap
I'm endlessly trying

to gnaw my leg
out of.

I need sharper
teeth.

Whenever I catch people
staring at me,
I always see a look of fear
anxiously biting its nails
in their eyes.

& as much as it hurts
seeing this look of nail-biting fear
over & over,
I can't help but inwardly laugh

because even though
I might look like Mein Kampf
walking through a spider web

these people will never know
I'm a million times more scared of them
than they are of me.

The sun
is an apathetic heat lamp
& you're the dried up,
dead-looking
7/11 hot dog
rotating underneath it,
    endlessly sizzling
the whispered confession of,

    Yeah… I been here
since they opened the place
back in '85

    & I don't really want me either,
I guess.

On my way walking to the train,
    I stopped, sat down on the sidewalk
    & pulled a bloody piece of bubble wrap
out of my left sneaker.

My sneaker had a hole on the inside
& a sharp piece of plastic (?)
cut into my heel whenever I walked.

The bubble wrap was something
I'd grabbed at work & stuffed into
the back of my sneaker in an attempt
to try & cushion the constant stabbing.

I looked at the bloody piece of
bubble wrap & saw the bubbles
were popped so I crumpled it up
& threw it in the gutter.

Then I began limping my way
back to the train.

Sometimes I think
I'm the most beautiful person
in the world.

The housing-impaired woman's
street-painted face
read like an obituary
for a brutally murdered
swing set.

I can't forgive them
for everything
they've taken away
either.

I don't think we're
supposed to.

The monsters don't live
    underneath your bed
        anymore
    because you let them grow up
    & eat you out of house
        & home.

    When the monsters smile at you,
    you can see pieces of
    your childhood bedroom
    in their gnarled, yellow teeth.

    "You have some of my childhood
    stuck in your teeth," you say.

    "I know," the monsters always reply

    & then tussle the bald spot
    on top of your head
    as if you still have hair there.

P utting your soul in a shoebox,
poking holes in the shoebox
so your soul can breathe,

dropping some blades of grass inside
so your soul can eat,

dropping in a couple pogs & slammers
for your soul to play with,

kissing the shoebox's top & whispering,
"I'll come back for you when it's safe..."
before sliding your soul underneath your
childhood bed, stepping outside & then
throwing yourself down their apocalyptic
stairs made of dirty, groping hands,

knowing damn well
you'll never see your soul again

but also knowing deep down,
"It's better this way."

Standing on the street,
        refusing to subserviently roll out
        my red carpet tongue to the rim
of winter's asshole,
I look around at all these people
walking, talking,
standing, breathing,
living,
        some willingly,
        some unwillingly,
                some totally indifferent to the sun
                & its horrible posture,
        & all I can think is,
            I really hope this works out...
in regards to me

& them

& us

& the sky above
the color of a dead
vacuum cleaner.

S creaming cardboard like,

"Hi. My name is Matt.

I'm eighteen years old

and my life sucks.

Please help."

ii.

An expensively-dressed
young woman
stops on the sidewalk
next to a housing-impaired kid
sitting behind a big piece
of screaming cardboard.

The expensively-dressed
young woman
quickly fixes her hair, smiles
then takes a selfie.

It's her one-millionth selfie
& balloons fall down from
the sky in grand celebration.

The balloons bounce off her
& accidentally bounce off
the housing-impaired kid
but the housing-impaired kid
doesn't feel them.

At some point

during her celebration
he transformed into a mailbox
   or garbage can
      or lamppost
         or parking meter
            etc. etc.
& now all that's left of him
is his screaming cardboard
still screaming,

screaming,
   "If cardboard screams
but no one is around
to hear it
does the cardboard
make a sound?"

Then the expensively dressed
young woman
turns on her high heels,
walks away without looking back
   &, in doing so,
she gives the screaming cardboard
its answer.

The next time
you put on your expensive suit
&/or designer dress,

remember we're all nothing more
than tiny, black prayers
coming from the far-away,
open mouths
of dead subway rats,

momentarily lost
but still heading to the exact same emptiness
that waits for us like a cosmic-sized
McDonald's bag with all of the fries
already snatched from the grease-coated
bottom.

The most accurate reflection
          of human beings
are those dumpster-looking
donation bins left in the far backs
of grocery store parking lots.

You don't need X-ray vision to see
how completely empty they are
inside,

     except for the lone candy bar wrapper
lying intruder-like in the bottom,

trying to grow like a pale flower.

I handed him the last
three dollars I had
& when he took the money
from my hand
he tried thanking me with his eyes
—he wanted to thank me
with his eyes—
but too much had already been
taken away for him to do so.

His eyes were a kind, feminine blue
& he wore a skull cap
& the streets had groomed his beard
into a charcoal mishap.

I never asked him
his name
though.

I should've asked him
his name.

It would've been like
giving him another
three dollars.

Probably more.

Wounds & hang-ups
       float above your head
       like gaping, black balloons
       cobwebbed to dark matter crumbs
       of your childhood.

       Despite their inflated,
       car crash appeal,
       the balloons make you invisible.

       You don't know why
       you're surprised over this

       but you always are.

i.

The man standing
    next to me on the A train
    keeps taking off his sneakers
    & then putting them back on
    & then taking them off
    & then putting them back on.

He's either shitfaced
or just really misses/likes
the sight of his socks.

ii.

I just noticed that
his socks have little,
yellow ducks on them.

It's really
anyone's game
now.

Young girl —

Five-feet tall,
hair the color of a window
looking out at the brick wall
of an adjacent apartment building,
& almost pretty the same way
a ten-dollar bottle of wine
you paid for with exact change
is almost tasty.

You'll do for tonight,

"Be yourself"
is horrible advice
to give someone

who wants to make friends.

Being yourself
will never make you friends
but dumbing yourself down
with a generic, mass-appealing
personality
that consists of nothing more than
doing yoga, going to the gym,
watching sports,
"I love to travel!"
"I love to laugh!"
your Netflix queue,
the iTunes top one-hundred
& morals & political beliefs
mindlessly compiled from headlines
& Facebook posts/memes
will make you a shit-ton
of friends.

If you want friends,
don't be yourself.

Be them.

& after you've lynched everything
black & gooey & unique
that screams inside you,
I'll be the one wearing
a (Batman) party hat
& shooting spitballs at their

collective corpse,

vandalizing what could've been,

vandalizing what was supposed to be,

vandalizing what you were too weak
to hold onto
in fear of being alone.

& I will too.

I've got no friends
& all the fucking time
in the world.

I have feelings like redundant
    game show prizes,
                    like redundant
    game show prizes.

    They never seem to get you
    anywhere,
        do they?

    There   is
    nowhere to go.

    There's only the emptiness
    a free lifetime supply
    of Burger King couldn't fill.

    Please don't look at me
    when I spin in circles
    & chase my imaginary tale.

    I'm trying to tire myself out
    so I can finally rest my head
    on this beautiful, apolitical concrete
    & fall asleep,

    so I can unconsciously color in
    the great uncolorable coloring book
    by not coloring it in
    at all.

    Break your crayons like bones
    & laugh,
    is something that echoes in my head
    frequently

24

   & I look forward to the warm,
pungent, golden shower day
when I grow a pair of balls
big & iron enough
to listen.

Your greatest achievement in life
was that sand castle you built
by yourself when you were

five years old.
Not because the sandcastle
was awesome
but because of the simple
yet massive amount of joy
that building it brought you
even though you knew
sooner or later
some high-tided, son of a bitch-wave
was going to come along
& destroy it.

Just when you think
    there's nothing in this world
    worth fighting for,
    you see a rat on the subway tracks,

      gnawing surgically
      on an unidentifiable piece
      of garbage,
        making you nod to yourself
      & think,

          Okay Dr. Rat…

            Okay…

i.

The man in the booth
across from me in McDonald's
wears a light purple bandana,
sits with perfect
statuesque posture
& swipes his finger across his iPad
like he is frosting a cake.

I feel like thanking him

but I don't know
why.

ii.

I've figured
it out.

It's because his existence
reads like the fragmented
sentence,

"Gentle, one-man
lavender parade."

nother day,
  unsanitary & unchosen,

  left to the quiet devices
  of self-consolation
  as all the beautiful people
  of the world hold conversations
  while stripping naked
  & getting into bed together.

  I feel just like a sewer rat
  who tied a tiny "Get Well Soon!"
  balloon around one of its legs

  only to drop dead seconds later.

For Courtney,

People
are too complicated
& love
is too simple

& most days
the slaughter is just too goddamned
hard to watch

like an angel

slowly
slitting her throat
with her own halo,

smiling
at you
as she leaks.

Smiling.

A punk rock safety pin
    that reads Brautigan,
    watches M. Monroe movies

    & pets stray cats
drops into a human-shaped chalk outline
but can't be heard over the lazy,
wide-eyed & waiting silence
of the gutted crime scene
wanting to be told what to do,
what to think,
what to feel,
what to like,
what to wear.

The human-shaped chalk outline
takes a selfie in its new summer dress
from H&M & posts the picture
to its Instagram account.

The picture gets over two-hundred likes within
the first two minutes of being posted.

The safety pin sighs.

It hopes some pigeons
come strutting by
soon
so it'll have something real
to watch & admire.

She & I met in a small, docked boat
made of coughing & mucus.

She wore lacy, pastel flats on her feet
& I asked her to take them off.

She did & then I took my cock out
& began masturbating as I looked at
her perfect ginger feet.

"Men have two settings," she said with her toes
by stretching them like pale, unpainted xylophones.
"Horny & hungry."

Shortly after, I came on her feet.

It was a warm, wonderful snowfall
that made both of us smile.

"Do you wanna row to Taco Bell?"
I asked her.

A heart filled with
a dead hamster-emptiness
cartwheels across

the grassy landscape of my youth
like a little girl doing cartwheels
across her front lawn
on the last day of summer.

The little girl's parents
watch from the window,

arguing over which one of them
is going to break the news
that the family cat has torn
her pet hamster to shreds.

The forgotten crumbs
        of your devoured childhood
        didn't know what to do
        so, lonely & scared,
        they dressed up as ghosts.

    Your ghost crumbs
    haunt you regularly,
            seven days a week
                (Monday through Monday),
        like frisbees & Nerf footballs
        stuck in the rain gutters
        of your mind,

        begging you
        to come outside
        & save them/play with them
        before it's too late.

        If it isn't already.

The older I get
the more I begin to sadly realize
I'll never be the leader of an
unholy legion of cats that help me
take over this shit world.

Maybe growing up just means
not lying to yourself
anymore.

I finally said, "To hell with this shit,"
ripped off my uncomfortable skin
& tied it around my neck like a cape.

Ran up & down the sidewalks
with my arms stretched in front of me
& made swishing-flying air sounds
with my mouth.

Everyone on the streets stopped
& stared at me like I was crazy
& generally looked disgusted
over what I was doing.

Not because I was inside-out-naked
or because of the trail of blood
I was leaving behind.

But because of how extremely
    unadult-like
I was behaving.

Lucky for me
I was too busy saving the world
to care.

L
ike an action figure
being bent & manipulated
by a large pair of invisible hands

that just finished an intense
two-hour masturbation session
jerking off its invisible dick
in an air conditioningless, windowless
basement on the hottest day of summer,
you walk down the sidewalk
on your way to work,
kicking a crumpled
Dunkin Donuts cup while wondering
how many of your daily actions
are authentically your own.

You do the math in your head,
come to a rough answer
& then accidentally kick
the empty Dunkin Donuts cup
into the street.

You walk over to the curb,
pick up the cup,
drop it back on the sidewalk
& then carefully,

softly,

slowly,
kick it the rest of your way
to work,

ignoring the smarmy
sun

as it laughs at you
like a mid-2000's
Tom Cruise.

When I got on the C train, there
were plenty of seats to choose from
but I chose a seat in the corner,
      the one with a dirty diaper
on the seat next to it.

The dirty diaper was full & smelled
& had The Cookie Monster on it
& I was fine with all of this because
I knew the dirty diaper would become
a force field against other people
sitting next to/standing near me
when the train finally began filling up.

I saw the only other guy in the train car
looking at me.

He stared at me like I was crazy.

I stared back at him like, "Hey, man.

You save your soul your way

& I'll save my soul my way."

Chewing the asphalt-flavored
    bubblegum that is your mind,
    you watch the crumb-filled 6 Train
pull out of the station
like an arthritic, rusty old man
pulling his pants up after
a twenty-minute, hard-stooled shit.

& then you're alone again,
aging in a musty, gradual silence,

    your mind quickly losing flavor

& still with no idea
where
it wants you to be.

A hospital bracelet becomes the noose
        around the neck of summer
        as the leafless trees sway around me
   in uncomfortable laughter.

   I want to tell Laura what's going on
   but she's moving to Miami
   where the weather is tanned & buff
   & the men are warm and sunny
   & where I'm over twelve-hundred
   miles away

   just like she wants me.

A pack of cigarettes with a ponytail
    coughs into its fist four times in a row
    then spits some phlegm
into the palm of its hand.

The pack of cigarettes with a ponytail
looks at the phlegm in its hand
like the phlegm is sexy—
    like the phlegm could be Miss July
    in a phlegm bathing suit calendar—
then licks the phlegm off its hand
& continues reading its book.

It's 9:30 A.M.

There's around twelve hours of day
left to kill
    & after that exhibit of true love,
you know it's all downhill
from here.

A housing impaired man
        wraps his McDonald's hash brown
        in a cheap paper napkin & then gently
        massages it, absorbing the grease.

After he absorbs most of the grease,
he puts his hash brown down & mutters,
        "Ketchup…I need ketchup…"
then stands up, shuffles outside
& never comes back.

An hour later, a McDonald's employee
comes over to clean his table,
gathers everything he left behind
& dumps it in the trash.

"Shit…" I say to myself out loud

feeling the oval-shaped hash brown
at the bottom of the garbage,

waiting on the ketchup that will never come

just like so many of us
I've come to know.

Pair after pair
of mad, whirling
chainsaw eyes
cut through these beautiful,
frozen people
filled with forgotten about
soft, creamy, nougaty
middles.

It's a gruesome thing
to watch

but god damn,

the gnawing,
Christian silence
it makes
is even worse.

S omeplace, somewhere,

some person is screaming
in soundless, Hoover Dam(n)-like
pain.

A small, yellow bird
flies in out of nowhere
& lands on the scream.

    Stunned,
the scream freezes in place
& the person stops & stares
& no one knows what to do

except the small, yellow bird,

pecking at its feathers
like the action of a small child
mindlessly picking their nose
in public.

Innocence lost
like watching a bright red balloon
float into a sky the color
of "no recess,"

taking its time,

ascending in gut wrenching
slow motion.

When the balloon completely
vanishes from sight,
your craned neck snaps.

Start all over
again.

I found them in a dumpster
    at work —a twelve-pack of Magic Grow
    Safari Animals.

I remembered them from when
I was a kid. These capsule-things
you dropped into water that grew
into animal-shaped sponges.

After work, I walked around the city
& dropped the capsules into puddles
leftover from the rainstorm earlier
that morning & then walked away before
I got a chance to watch them grow.

I imagined a man waiting to cross the street
looking down & seeing a yellow monkey-shaped
sponge in the puddle by his feet & something
dead inside of him almost smiling.

I feel like planting
those lost seeds of innocence
was the closest I've ever come
to truly loving myself
as an adult.

Most likely because it was the closest
I've ever come to truly feeling
like a kid again.

On these slow-dying
    Sunday afternoons,
    you haunt me like persuasive

    frozen pizza crust
    refusing to be digested
    & cross over.

    I don't care
    we were no good
    for each other.

    I miss you.

I just watched an old man
   throw away an empty cup of coffee
   as if he were dropping a rose
   onto the casket of his deceased wife.

   I feel both jealous of
      & sorry
   for him.

Having sex with someone you don't love
feels like kissing Lucy Lawless
when you really just want to be making out
with Xena: Warrior Princess.

Happy 90th, "Mmmmm girl,"

Sitting in a rocking chair
that she rocked back & forth
like a rocking horse,
she spoke to me with the voice
of a spotlessly cleaned
wine glass that smoked cigarettes.

Her hair was the color of singing snow
& her eyes were the color of sadness
doing a headstand.

I sat across from her in a rocking chair
of my own & we drank tea
& talked about nothing
& laughed about nothing.

Her laugh was like listening to a flower
trying not to laugh.

It came from the same part of her
that turned her rocking chair
into a rocking horse.

"Imagination"
is a childish, frowned upon word
that needs to wash its hands,

brush its teeth & go to bed.

Until it makes someone
millions of dollars.

Then it's called "genius"
& can stay up as late
as it fucking wants
eating bowl after bowl
of party cake ice cream.

I grew up last night
     when I looked into the sky
     & (finally) realized no one
     was coming for me.

It made a dinging sound

like golden elevator doors
closing in my face.

Underneath fingernails,
  beside the dirt & grime that's
  curled up like sleeping black cats
  exhausted from a fruitless day
  spent hunting—

  this is where the American Dream
  goes to die.

Cleaning your nails
     with a box cutter
          in public
is a really good way
to turn people's eyes
into birthday cakes
who just had their candles blown out
& are sitting in the dark
     alone & scared
wondering what the hell
is going to happen next.

A sky
like an enormous
Friedrich Nietzsche-looking
manhole cover
tries to explain your mind
to you.

You stand on the street,
    holding an ineffective umbrella
over your head like a regurgitated
question mark,

    missing the good ol' glory days
of depression

when all the sky
ever did
was rain on you.

Instead of going out on weekends
        you stay in, open your closet door
        & throw rainbow sprinkles at
the forehead of the apocalypse.

The apocalypse's forehead
is botoxed & taut,
    like a Hollywood trampoline,
& the rainbow sprinkles bounce off it
& into your mouth.

"You're going to ruin your dinner,"
a clay-sounding voice
says from the shadows.

"Good..." you say. "I hope I do,"

& then kid yourself by opening
a new package of rainbow sprinkles,

pretending this form
of childish self-defense
can go on forever.

S he closes her eyes
  & brushes the hair from her face
  like a newlywed clock
  that the sun sets itself
  & secretly masturbates to.

Holy shit...

I know she's performed this action
thousands of times in her life

but I'm just grateful I got
to see it once.

You used to think
	you had something
	to offer the world

but as you sit here at the edge
of your bruised limitations,
	alone,
marinating in your own
neanderthal stench,
		as you've done so many times
		before,
			as you'll do so many times
			in the future,

you're not even sure
if you have anything left
to offer yourself.

Decaying with grace.

"Pinkies up" as you sip on Drano.

Your insides were never
fashion-forward
to begin with.

My place in history —

inside an empty, cat hair-covered
Carlo Rossi wine jug
left beside a McDonald's dumpster
with a small cardboard plaque
that no one taking out the trash
ever stops to read
but says,

*Here lies the greasy, slothful,
cloud-like deeds
of HOMELESS...*

*The only starving artist
EVER
who somehow managed to
constantly put on weight.*

Staring at a foreclosed house
    that's been empty almost a year now,
    you wonder if you're the only person
    who looks at the lonely satellite dish
    stranded on the roof & feels sorry for it.

Maybe the dish & the chimney
will somehow become friends.

The echo of two dive bars
        discussing cigarette prices
        stares inside the darkened window

of dollar store sadness
rather than reflecting off the window
& returning with some kind of understanding
on this clammy-handed day
when all you feel is death
hanging in the closet
like an ugly, black sweater
your ex-girlfriend bought for you.

This morning I saw
a sun-bleached, flattened bird
matted into the street.

I tried flipping it over
with the spatula of my thoughts,
as if that would help
or somehow bring it back to life,
but the flattened bird
wouldn't budge.

Death is so much stronger than us
& our numerous
good intentions.

S itting in Wendy's,
   "Night Fever" by The Bee Gees
   plays from the speakers
   hidden in the ceiling.

The housing-impaired man
sitting at the table next to mine
begins shadow boxing
to the rhythm.

Something about it makes me
think back to a few hours ago,
when Lexi threw a Japanese garden
over her naked body & ran off
to the bathroom.

When I hold my fingers up to my nose,
I can still smell her on them.

Her scent is like
the housing-impaired man's
shadow boxing.

Sometimes the world
is so beautiful
it hurts.

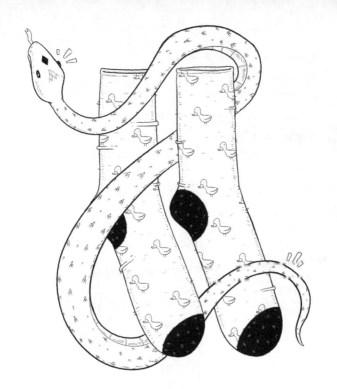

Sitting in a cold, underwater stairwell
    & drenched in drowning
    as you wait to go back to work,

you stare at a dead cockroach
like it's a belly up funeral procession
that's arrived at the cemetery thought,

"The only real way to kill time
is to not appreciate it."

Her hair was the color
        of embarrassed ketchup
        & the way she poured cream
into her coffee
reminded me of someone
petting a stray cat.

"Marry me," I wanted to say to her.

"Fuck me
with your blushing gentleness
forever."

Anal bead blue eyes
    slid their way inside
    our Sunday mornings.

When the eyes
came back out
they were never brown.

Only blue,

        baby-wiped clean
        & hopeful,

as if love
could go on
forever.

Wearing a large, heavy necklace
made of clock testicles
in memoriam of all the hours
that had to be castrated in exchange
for those singular, beautiful hours
(few & far between)
where everything was finally left
just as it should be —

simple, perfect, painless

& intact.

A hole inside of you
like a rip
in a black garbage bag.

Even when your head's above
the wild, white roses
you still feel it.

A repeated tap on the shoulder
in this dragged out process of loss
saying, "Hey, congratulations!

You made it.

You're human."

She jiggled her foot up & down
    with her shoe hanging from her toes
    like a lynched sunrise.

    I wanted to bathe in it
    somehow.

        This is where
    imagination
    generally leaves you —

    lonely, dirty, disappointed
    & blue-balled
    as fuck,

    wanting more even though
    you've had none
    to begin with.

After staring into a puddle on the street
    & seeing the reflection of a bottle
    of bum wine throwing a temper tantrum

in the toy aisle of a Walmart
staring back at you,
    you sigh.

Your sigh sounds like
the eight bucks you have left in your
decomposing wallet
sighing.

"Might as well spend it
on soft tacos," you say out loud

before remembering
you're alone.

Two empty shopping carts
        pressed up against each other
        in the after hours of a
        supermarket parking lot—

        I know love like this exists
        but can't even vaguely remember
        what it feels like.

Dressed like a vinyl record,
　　she sat crammed in-between
　　two vaudevillian, walrus impressions

　　with a punk rock grace that
　　leaked unanimously from her eyes.

The only thing she carried with her
was a cardboard tube
with CUNT BULLET
written on it in dark red ink
that seemed to be squinting in
the ugly, fluorescent subway light.

Right then & there,
I knew that was how
I wanted to die someday.

Especially
if the cunt bullet
was coming from her,

　　Point-blank in the forehead,

　　the back of my skull exploding
like an underage wet dream
running out the back door
of a bar going up in flames.

Middle-aged,
hair like a haunted hayride
& eyes like haggard combat boots,

a female McDonald's employee
looks at her paycheck
like it's a flaming bag of dog poo
she's trying to stomp out
with her haggard, combat boot-eyes.

I kind of want to have
sex with her

a lot.

For Kurt,

Looking up
The Empire State Building's skirt,
her big, concrete camel toe
calls me back to a home
I never had.

Fucked up, forgotten
    & still breathing deep-fried
    teenage angst,
I miss the ignorant,
womb-like comfort in being alone
more than ever.

When you fall asleep on the subway
your hair becomes beautiful drapes
of bacon that light themselves on fire
& your mouth hangs open
like an indirect & mischievous
run-on sentence hailing a cab
to the mouth of the boyfriend
I know you have.

I wanted to tell you this in person
but you were asleep

& you're also a stranger

& you're also, also
the kind of girl who looks like
she carries pepper spray.

The prettiest redhead
I've ever seen —

she's sitting in Grand Central
eating a salad as if she's setting
a rat trap on her tongue.

I'm sitting across from her
trying not to stare,

thinking,
Holy shit...

I'd love to die
in her mouth.

i.

Crater-faced, unrhythmic
    & silently bellowing
    like a midnight scream
    tiptoeing across a floor
    covered in shattered glass
    frowns,

I'm ninety eight percent sure
I'll be sleeping alone
tonight.

ii.

I just discovered
a long, stray hair
growing out the side
of my ear.

Ninety-nine percent
sure.

A lonely immigrant
    waiting, hoping for work
    sits on the sidewalk
    next to an empty rocking chair.

He looks like an exhausted
Chaplin pratfall on loop
but the empty rocking chair
isn't laughing. The empty rocker
hasn't had an ass sit on its face
since LBJ was in office & lost
its sense of humor somewhere around
the end of The Vietnam War.

But the lonely immigrant
keeps trying anyway,

sitting there with the rocking chair,
    alone,
        falling over & over,

& the only applause he receives
is the sound of my footsteps walking by,
    dissolving our time together
like the end credits to
"Stand By Me."

He deserves
more.

A housing-impaired man
    lies on the grass in Union Square Park
    like a stringless, sunburnt violin
    trying to play itself.

    No one else can hear the song
    he's unable to play but,
      listening carefully enough,
    warm, jagged shards of it
    reflect off the sunlight & pour
    into my ears like cheap, wounded beer.

    I lie down in the grass
    like a slightly buzzed Carnegie Hall
    & stare up at the oozing green
    canopy of leaves,

        grateful,
      consoled
    & hoping
    this is what it feels like
    to die.

Stared at by eyes
        made of unscrubbed porcelain,
        I was flushed into the background
        without a sound.

I used to think this was the worst thing
that ever happened to me, but now,
watching everyone live their lives
from this binocular distance,
        & seeing them all conducted by
        the vibrator-shaped baton
        of loneliness,

I can't help but smile

& feel like the luckiest
shithead
alive.

The year was unusually cold
           & prophetic in the monster mask it wore
           & everyone walked around with scared
sticks up their asses that also had scared
sticks up their asses.

I remained obscure
& stared down at sidewalks.

The sidewalks liked to pretend
they were gray area night skies,
    their black tar stars
burning like old fashioned tube TVs
& burping up a static that drowned out
all selfish traces of the world.

It was the same thing on every channel
but it licked your wounds clean with
a humanity that all humans seemed
unsuspiciously
        absent of.

R ich sits alone
in the McDonald's dining room
& picks up his small cup
of coffee
and presses it to his lips
and takes small sips
from it.
Like
really small sips.
Like
the coffee has to last him
the rest of his life kind of
small sips.
Rich is 65
now
or somewhere
around the age
of 65.
His sips of his coffee
are so small
that Rich will finally finish
his coffee
around the age of 102
or so
unless, of course,
he dies first.
But I really hope Rich doesn't
die first.
I really feel like Rich
deserves to finish
this cup of coffee
of his,
even if it takes him

37 years
to do so.
If he does die
first,
    however,
Rich's unfinished cup of coffee
will attend his funeral.
I will be there
too.
I have a sad feeling
it will just be me,
Rich's cup of coffee
& Rich's dead body
at the funeral.
Rich's cup of coffee
will wear a small, black veil
to the intimate gathering.
I won't be able to see
its face
but I'll know the cup of coffee
is silently crying
behind its veil.
When it's able
to compose itself enough,
    when it somehow gets its crying
    that I can't see
    but know is there
    under control,
Rich will be eulogized
by his cup of coffee.
It will stand there
in front of the coffin,
    the coffin towering over it,
        dwarfing it

&, consequently, making the cup of coffee
feel even smaller
than ever,
but somehow,
Rich's cup of coffee will summon strength
from somewhere inside it
&,
    through a powerful silence
    emanating from the cup
    of coffee itself,
Rich's cup of coffee
will begin eulogizing
its lost friend...
"Not only have I lost
my best friend,
    but I've lost
a piece of myself,
    & a piece
of myself
I'll never get back
either.
I will forever miss
the way
he would pick me up
like there was no other
cup of coffee
in the entire world
for him
& the way
that the touch of his big,
soft lips
reassured me
that I was
the only cup of coffee

in the world
for him.
He took small sips
out of me,
one
after the other,
    after the other,
        after the other,
but it never felt like
he was emptying
me.
Not once
did it ever feel like
he was emptying me
but, yet,
    somehow,
filling me…
    Always filling me.
& then,
    when he was done
    sipping from me,
        me filling him
        & him filling me,
he'd gently put me back down
on the table,
    never too far
    outta reach,
but always just close enough
to be picked up
& sipped from
again.
That was our life
together
& it was a simple life

full of simple beauties
in an over complicated world
full of ugliness.
Goodbye,
    Rich.
I love you.
You were the
man…"
Then I
will begin crying.
I will cry because
even though I didn't know Rich
too well
I'm also not a heartless monster
& I know true love
when I see
true love.
But Rich
isn't dead yet.
Rich is still
very much alive,
    sitting contently
with his cup of coffee
& me,
    I am sitting here
watching him sip
his cup of coffee
like some kind of creeper,
    but learning
    so much…
Some guys
climb mountains,
others
go out and bang

as much pussy
as possible,
others
build empires
in search of power
but some guys,
    perhaps even
    the braver ones,
just sit in McDonald's
& sip on a cup of coffee
that will take them
37 years
to finish.

ACKNOWLEDGMENTS

Endless thanks to Leza, Christoph, Eve,
DRP & Lexi. xoxo

ABOUT THE AUTHOR

Homeless lives in New York City. He is the author of the novel "This Hasn't Been a Very Magical Journey So Far" (Expat Press) and the short story/poetry collection "Please Buy This Book So I Can Feel Validated & (Finally) Love Myself" (House of Vlad).

If you'd like to reach him, you can find Homeless nestled on the virtual streets of obscurity at:

instagram.com/xoxohomeless
twitter.com/xoxohomeless

WE PUT THE LIT IN LITERARY

CLASHBOOKS.COM

TWITTER

IG

FB

@clashbooks

Email

clashmediabooks@gmail.com

Publicity

McKenna Rose

clashbookspublicity@gmail.com

CPSIA information can be obtained
at www.ICGtesting.com
Printed in the USA
BVHW030747180721
612164BV00024B/169

9 781944 866921